Unclenched:
A passive fist's manifesto

new poems by
Joseph Nicks

Copyright © 2021 by Joseph Nicks

Unclenched: a passive fist's manifesto
First Edition Copyright © 2022

ISBN 978-1-7363722-5-8

Published by Blue Jay Ink
Ojai, California
bluejayink.com

Book Design by Blue Jay Ink
Cover art by Ojai Digital

Credits:
Photo for The Horizontal Forest by Eugene Nekrasov
Photo for The Eternal Nocturning Of Earth by hareluya

This is MagPie Book #20.
Visit josephnicks.com for a complete list of
Magnesium Pie publications.

One-fourth of the proceeds from the sale of these
books is contributed to a fund that benefits the
following organizations:

The American Cetacean Society
Bat Conservation International
Black Mamba Anti-Poaching Unit
International Bird Rescue
Panthera.org

*when my fist clenches, crack it open
before I use it and lose my cool
and when I smile, tell me some bad news
before I laugh and act like a fool*
— Pete Townshend, 1971

*well, I'm accustomed to a smoother ride
or maybe I'm a dog who's lost his bite
I don't expect to be treated like a fool no more
I don't expect to sleep through the night*
— Paul Simon, 1990

Table of Contents   page

1 The Powder-Blue Twilight
The Beleaguered Bleed Of Evening	10
"Don't Let The Morning Come For Me"	11
The Endless Now	12
The Fifteen Commandments Of Survival	14
I Believe I Have The Floor	15
Another "We're All In This Together"	16
Some Sequestered Questions	17
A Question Within A Question	17
The Great Equalizer	18
Days Upon Days	19
I'd Like To Think	20
I Long For Longer Days	22
The Quiet Now	24
A Decade And A Day	25

2 The Horizontal Forest
For All That Lives And Eyes	28
Walled-In Pond	29
Our Own Air Looms On The Horizon	30
Terrestrial Anthr-apology	32
Manifest Density	34

3 The Eternal Nocturning Of Earth
According To Pall	38
No Wake Zone	39
Post-prehensile	40
When	41
One Of These Nights	42
On Waking Up Again	43

Table of Contents   **page**

4 Fuck *Me*!
A Small Unswallowable Certainty	46
Nognosis	48
Just A Poem	50
If You've Learned Anything At All	52
Whose Cider You On?	53
The Fall	54
Days Of Infamy	57

5 Red Shift
Man, I'm Not Even Here	60
Out Here In The Bewilderness	61
Subsiding	62
Dichotomous?	63
October And Elsewhen	64
Some Wear In PST	66
If Only For A Moment	68
Approaching Solstice	69
Leaving Lapeer	70
Thawlessness	72
After Ours	74

Some Notes On A Sister No More...   77

Appendix: a chronology of these poems   78

1
The Powder-Blue Twilight

The Beleaguered Bleed Of Evening

on such long-shadowed
waning afternoons
not one of us seems able
to explain exactly why

the heart grows heaviest
in the deepening
and dying down of day

or how the settling
of the landscape
into darkness
one more time

can act as
such a balm
for so many
ancient wounds

"Don't Let The Morning Come For Me",

I used to lie awake and pray
way back when I was prone to praying
in my myopic Lutheran faith and helplessness

of course it seized me every day
in a perverse reverse of Horace's
carpe diem

it showered me and scrubbed me,
clean-shirted, shaved and shod me
and flung me out the door

into the gaping jaws
of grunt-work peonage
that devours everything
from your bones
to your blood
to your breath

the whistle blew
but none too soon –
I limped home
bruised by afternoon

in lingered intermingling
of ale-ment and affliction
and furtive glances at those thighs
uncaressed by more than eyes

inexplicably alive still on arrival,
my ink was bleeding
into intervening evening…

Joseph Nicks

The Endless Now

one   and so you run from the sun
deep into the night
but the faster and further you run
the sooner you see that same sun
in all its dreaded resplendent
comeuppance once again
cruelly shining in your face
and mocking your puny
and futile attempt to escape

two   in such a hurry to mature
you try to leave your green
and foolish youth behind
clambering up that hill
to reach the peak and
find out what it's all about
but when you get there
you'll be quick to realize
it's not what you'd
envisioned it to be
and the only direction
is downward
from now on

three   to elude all deathly thoughts
you hurtle headlong into life –
wide-open throttle and closing
on the dying that all living
must collide with down that road

four   you stagger from the past
with wasted days
and darkness in your wake,
a landscape steeped
in sorrow and regret –
forever hopeward bound,
you cast your eyes
on the disquieting horizon
and freeze in the only moment
you can do anything about

The Fifteen Commandments Of Survival

01   Be useful.
02   Stay out of everyone's way, including your own.
03   Try not to get yelled at.
04   Keep your senses tuned to your surroundings.
05   Never stop trying to *understand* this shit – don't let your "why"s be clogged by mere "because"s.
06   Do your best not to harm any living organism.
07   Concern your head, your heart, and your hands with the plight of others.
08   Pay for your mistakes.
09   Learn from your mistakes.
10   Second-guess and double-check everything you think, say, and do.
11   Don't drive into any place you can't walk back out of.
12   Travel light – be as self-contained as possible.
13   Don't go to sleep on momentum; don't stay awake in inertia.
14   Never count on luck, divine intervention, or the milk of human kindness.
15   Don't expect to be rewarded for any of this – temporally or eternally.

I Believe I Have The Floor,

I mean I pace its every inch —
and the walls of up to maybe
six or seven feet of reach

sometimes I even have the windows —
unshuttered, unobstructed
reminding me the world goes on without me

but the ceiling's just too high for me
to do anything but peer into its blankness

and the door, if I could find it
after so many sequestered semesters,
would surely be completely rusted shut

Another "We're All In This Together"

well, there it is

another morning greets this hope-starved world

and, lucky us, we survived *another* night

don't know why – we just did

never mind about all those who didn't

just be glad you've been given *another* day

that you can do next to nothing with

Some Sequestered Questions

Where has "the voice of reason" gone?

Isn't there more than one?

Hasn't there always been?

How can we even hear it
now above the 5G din?

Just how uncommon
has the "common sense"
become?

A Question Within A Question

How often do you ask yourself,
"what do I really *know*?"?

The Great Equalizer

when everyone is wearing one,
individuality overshadowed
by concern for the common good

when what's best for everybody
seems to be what's on the forefront
of most everybody's mind

when no one of us feels better,
more privileged or entitled
than the rest

when more hands are lent
than borrowed,
then perhaps we'll end up
human after all...

Days Upon Days

don't eat 'til you're hungry
don't sleep 'til you tire
fight when you have to
love when you can

and think on every word
you hear or say

try to reason with your anger
feel everybody's fear
do your crippled best to ease
as much of all this
suffering as you can

and commingle in the sorrow
that is survivorship's reward

just make damn sure
you've done all you can
before you finally call it a day
and crack another beer

I'd Like To Think

that I could somehow be
more like Jesus or Gandhi
or MLK

but alas I'm just another
poor fucked-up bastard
who's tried my futile best
to rise above all the
resentment I feel
for the way the world turns
and turns away from itself
and turns back upon itself

that one day I wouldn't feel
such anger and hatred
for all the thugs and bullies
and takers and con-men out there

but what am I gonna do –
love them and all the suffering
that they cause???

after all, isn't love a form
of nurture – and why in the world
would we want to nurture
their hatred with our love???

that John was right when he said
love is the answer
and you know that for sure

but we can't go on like this
in one-sided unrequited love
turning and turning our other cheeks
until we've run out of cheeks to turn

laying the grisly foundation
for the few of frivolous privilege
and the money-muscle-mongers
who gain their traction
from the compaction
of layer upon layer upon layer
of our allegiance, our bones, our blood

that I could think of a way
to not always be feeling
so god damned bad

but if I found I didn't feel
that way about a planet
as fucked up as this one
do you honestly think that
I'd really be thinking at all?

I Long For Longer Days

those bright but hazy
watermelon-summered days
of clueless youth
when we still had to
spit out the seeds
and we didn't care
that the sticky juice
was dripping off our chins

our lives were so full
that breakfast seemed
a distant past
by the rolling around
of bedtime

we were so much smarter
than our phones
they stayed at home
and we were on our own
for most of the day

our search engine was the
Dewey Decimal System
and there were no annoying
Alexas or Siris or Cortanas
around to pretend to help us
with our homework or our chores
or try to show us how to
dress ourselves and pee

we didn't need an Xbox
to teach us how to play
and we didn't text
or twitter —
we just talked
and hand-wrote letters
to each other

and brother, sister,
you don't need an app
for that

The Quiet Now

if I could just stop dying
for a moment
and breathe the wind
that sweeps across the fields,

look deep into
the canopy and see
the forest for the trees
and the trees for the forest,
green so richly thrust against the blue
and white of clouds,

feel the brash and unapologetic
purples, yellows, oranges
that paint the pallid desert
when the winter rains subside,

sense the flesh and blood
lain low here while it can be,
starvation played
against predation
as urgent life-clocks
tick away the seasons,

and immerse myself in the living
that flows so irretrievably downstream

A Decade And A Day

seems like it must have lasted
for a decade and a day
but by the time it really registered,
it was far too late
to do a whole lot about it

and deep here in our middle life,
the sky outside looks fine
but for the ominous horizon

lying-to among our labors,
a scant few of us take notice –
and that's precisely what keeps
keeping us from ease

as foreboding and regret
conspire to fend off
all forgetfulness and hope

though it grows harder to discern
between a decade and a day,
you still can hear the storm a-coming
from a hundred miles away

2
The Horizontal Forest

For All That Lives And Eyes

from catamount to cachalot
and eft to dhole to waxwing

from terrapin to pipistrelle
and numbat, gemsbok, turnstone

basking in the biosphere,
I have looked into
those living eyes
and seen my kinship there –
and if for just one lonely moment
I belonged to something larger

from gentoo to thylacine,
spring peeper to tamandua

from bushmaster to hellbender
chuckwalla, chuck-will's-widow

adrift in twilit necroscapes,
I have looked into
those dying eyes –
at some point
they go far away,
as if focusing on something
the still-living cannot see

Walled-In Pond

for *Trachemys scripta elegans*

I went down
to watch them
feed the waterfowl
with perhaps
their best of
intentions
and see sliders
bask invasively
at El Dorado Park

often the most common
chelonian species now —
in places where
they never used to be

it's hard to be too hard
on them in this rare
example of bio-poetic justice —
this is the red-ear's revenge
for all those soggy years of
soft-shelled confinement
in shallow unswimmable
plastic palm-treed prisons,
wearing dime-store sideshow
painted carapaces
as most of them so slowly
starved to death

Our Own Air Looms On The Horizon

life on a red-skied planet

step out of the halls
of natural history
into the bright and noisy
littleness of now
heady with eonic thoughts
of how all this came to be –
and wise to its
impending demise

the siliconistas
so smugly assume
their microsoftness
will allow us to
transcend our pedigree –
how biota on top of biota
survived undigitized
for nearly four billion years
is utterly inexplicable to them

but I saw new life spring
forth that spring
from a not-so-silent spring
in the now-vehicular valley
just east of here
and even then,

it didn't seem
to be as teeming
as it was
the epoch before

the sunsets sure are deeper,
more intense here
in the death throes of
tierra caliente
and its last gasps
of atmosphere (or at least
an air apparent)

just let your eyes roll over evening
to hesperian horizons –
you'll plainly see our legacy
smeared across the bloody firmament
to the delight of drunken sailors
and all the other erythrophiles

but in the morning
comes the warning
that the Martian ark
is leaving soon,
setting sail for redder pastures –
the 5G Apple saucers
gonna leave these "g"s behind,
no more will they be singin'
these old school blue planet blues

and I wish the fuck they'd go
and leave the rest of us alone

maybe then we can
finally get on with it –
the slow and low-tech salvage
of a greener, re-seasoned world

Terrestrial Anthr-apology

long after this unsustainable
infrastructure collapses
beneath the burden
of fecundity and affluence
and digital instability

the oozing oilfields,
damned-up rivers,
dried-out aquifers

the bird-and-bat-bashing windmills,
battery-burgeoning e-wasted landfills

the acres of solar panels
supplanting the plants,
impeding their photosynthetic necessity

the combusted troposphere,
de-ozonified stratosphere

the phosphorescent coastal dead zones,
deforested/defrosted Amazonia/Antarctica

the vanished worldwide megafauna

all will stand as silent testaments
to the ephemeral hyper-potency
of runaway hominism
whose viral expansion
from Pleistocene to Plastocene
left the far and wide terrestrium
styrofoaming at the seas

we could've lived less largely
but that's not the way we roll

of course it's going to take some healing, but
it certainly won't be a first for Earth
to have survived a mass extinction,
though never one of such intelligent design...

the eons will season
themselves again
and life will re-diversify
with no remembrance of those
naked, tailless, erectile monkeys
run amok for that horrible fortnight
so many ice ages ago

the grasses will
give it no glossing
and the worms won't
wonder who won

and in the understory
become the prologue
of stories yet to unfold,
a prideless proliferation
of unapologetic arthropods
will go on about their business
as they've been doing for
four hundred million years

Manifest Density

My little sister was born on Groundhog Day of 1960 and there were already 3 billion people on Earth.

By my graduation from high school in 1974, this number had risen to 4 billion.

Another billion were added by the time my first scrawlings were published as *Chronicide* in 1987.

Then a billion more came to share the air by the end of the last millennium.

Our accumulated billions numbered a decidedly unlucky "seven by 2011".

If you're keeping up with the math here, we've grown another billion every twelve-and-a-half years since 1960.

No one examining these trends has any doubt that the world population will reach 8 billion by 2023 (the Earth's sixth mass extinction will probably not yet have caught up with its perpetrator).

What should scare the living bejeezus out of us is that it took about 12 thousand years for us to number a billion by 1804, and then only 123 more years to reach our "second billion" milestone in 1927.

Damn, for a species that doesn't seem to be able to put two and two together, we sure do know how to multiply!

3
THE ETERNAL NOCTURNING OF EARTH

According To Pall

the unrelenting
hauntedness
of regret-stained
yesteryears

and the anxious
disquiescence
at the thought of
inescapable
misfutures

coalesce
in depths
immeasurable
and tortuous
half-sleep

until that same old
dreaded daycreep
lights the landscape
once again

reminding you
of dying
one more time

No Wake Zone

every morning when the sun
ignites the bruised
and bloody sky

I feel decidedly unlucky
that the night
has passed me by

and I'm obliged
to rise alive still
to occasions
I've no stake in
and put on that stupid
dayface I've come to despise

Post-prehensile

as not-so-naively-nigh
evening approaches,
all those things
we once couldn't
make sense of –
now they shine
so midnight-clear

sufficiently far away
from the blinding
white light of mid-day
and all that frenzied
juvenescence
gone so dizzily
down the drain,

what a tragedy
to grasp at last
what your hands
have lost their grip on

what a crime it is
that you can't have
your back back

When

when moonrise bathes
these prickly distances
and deepens each dimension,
only hinting at how much
you have ignored:

will you wonder how the night
can mean so many different things
to so many different people?

when the wind stirs distant memories
of a youth you never grasped
the urgency of:

will you continue to overthink
everything you do and don't
in your writhing leaping clawing
slow descent into tormentia?

when these many labored years
have sown such a stubborn
soreness in your sinew
and laid a leaden weariness upon you
that no amount of sleep
could ever erase:

will you marvel at the fact
that you still haven't
gotten used to
all of what you've seen
so many thousand times before?

One Of These Nights

I'll find a way
to stay asleep
and not have
to rise to reckon
with the dawn

I'll no longer
lie down a loser
and be expected to
wake up a winner

to the swelling
of that same old cock-
and-bull story
the morning seems
so bent on
unabashedly re-telling:

On Waking Up Again

though everyone who's died
will still be dead,
maybe today won't be so bad

though we've been losing
every battle,
perhaps today will be the day
we win the war

though they've been talking
the talk forever,
could this actually be the day
when someone listens?

go back to sleep, kid…

4
Fuck Me!

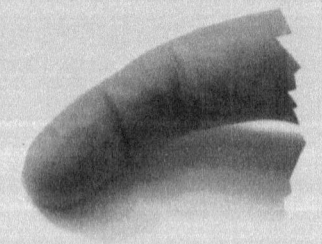

A Small Unswallowable Certainty

(that doesn't seem so small to me)

I guess it never
really leaves you
but you'd think
after all this time
you'd finally get
to wrapping your head
around it

my mom is really gone

my dad is really gone

my dog and my dog
are both surreally gone

another one of my friends
is really, really gone

and they are never,
never, never coming back

fall down and pound
upon the ground

and heed that primal urge
to howl out loud
and shout it to the clouds

death   death   death

death   death   death

death   death   death

shout it 'til it finally
begins to sink in

shout it like someday
you'll actually be able
to get over it

shout it 'til any god
that actually did exist
could no longer pretend
not to hear it

shout about
how profoundly
fucked up it is
that such a striving thriving
writhing thing as life
so inevitably inescapably
turns into death

Nognosis

Fuck, I know nothing about music.
Don't know why I even talk about it so much.
But the way it moves and moves me –
the way it wrings these tears so late at night,
far beyond the eyes of anyone
who'd ridicule my softitude
(or else break down, commence
to sobbing there themselves);
the way it lays another layer down
upon the stubborn mantle of resolve
that causes some of us so stupidly
to live to get up one more bleak,
faith-shaken day – well, I guess
I'll just keep going on about it.

Fuck, I don't know shit about cars.
Wonder why I think about them so much.
But there was once a day I had a wrench
to match my back and opposable thumbs
and I could keep an engine humming
and surging through the door of my garage
and out onto The Interstate that stretches
from Detroit to South California – and I guess
I'll just keep driving 'til they pry
my cold dead hands off of the wheel.

Fuck, I still don't know just how
we got so separated,
us and all the other animals –
breathing, drinking, eating, roaming,
sleeping, struggling with/against each other
just like us, they get by without all these
extraneous strata we the people pile up
on top of our living,
at the expense of all the living
(them and us).

Fuck, I still don't quite know how to say it –
these passages, they mostly write themselves.
I seem to always be just going about my business
when the words, they come a-thundering
from out of the "holy shit!" darkness,
hell-bent on trampling me dead. All I can do
is slap a few of them aside, deflecting them
to whatever piece of paper happens to be
lying nearby, surviving their onslaught
by the skin of my teeth – yet another night
that I won't have to yield
to the long-in-coming
sweet release of death.

Just A Poem

this is not a contest entry
this is not a slam –
it doesn't come with
bacon, ham, or sausage

it's not trying to rattle
some phony cage
or go for baroque
or beyond –
it doesn't even
have a cart to push

it's not hip,
hopped-up or hyped

it's not tattooed,
nipple-pierced,
spiky-orange-haired
or otherwise punkified

it's just a poem

the kind that's all
you have to turn to
in the washed-out afterhours
when another day
has laid your battered soul
flat out and sprawling in the dirt

the kind you mutter
under your breath
when the gods
and the traffic continue
to have their way with you

the kind that nips at your thinking
and bullies your conscience
until you relent
and put your pen to it
just to shut it up

the kind you cry out
in excruciation,
slash upon the page
to dim its blinding
inkless whiteness
so you can get some rest

the kind you can't blame
or feel gratitude toward

after all, it's just a poem

If You've Learned Anything At All

there will come a day
when you won't seem
so smart to you

and yet you'll cringe
when you look back
and plainly see
how much smarter
you are now
than you once were

and if you're really
that much smarter
than your phone,
your house, your TV,
or your safe
self-driving car:

you may come to realize
that all the gates and jobs
we've passed through,
all the musk we may've choked on,
every empty page we've overcome,
the besos on butt-cheeks and
bloodsucker burgermeisters
of billions and billions sold
in their attempts to both engorge
and subjugate us –

they may be luckier, more conniving,
and ultimately richer than us
but only as smart as we make them
by blindly embracing their stupidity

Whose Cider You On?

on the drunkenness of belonging

teams, teams, teams

tribes, tribes, tribes

clans, clans, clans

homeys, homeys, homeys

from political parties to drug cartels

from terrorist zealots to vigilante gun clubs

from HOAs to protection rackets

from conquering Christian crusaders to petty godless thugs

from the highbrow elite to the good old boy brotherhood

let's drink to our cronies at the expense of everyone else

does anyone think for themselves anymore?

is there anyone left with the guts to go it alone?

will no one stand in defiance of the mob?

The Fall

way back in 2020
that didn't mean what
it had meant in previous years

it had less to do with equinox
than equality, or more properly
equitability – a sustainable
condition in which everyone
reaped equally the selflessness
they'd sown

but first we'd have to outgrow the smoke
of chaos swirling thick and toxic
from the tyranny of tear gas
to the terrorism and torching
of vandals and looters hiding
behind the mask of righteous rebellion
in a world gone viral, volatile and vengeful

we'd have to see the error of our ways
and means and meanness most of all

we'd have to see that there's no difference
between oppressive laws
and lawless oppressors

we'd have to see that anarchy is a pipe dream
unless every single one of us is self-governed
by both reason and ethics
and that has never happened yet –
we shouldn't expect it ever will
(realism needs to temper our idealism)

we'd have to see that at least half
the information sailing down
that "information superhighway"
is second-hand at best
to downright groundless,
even connivingly contrived

we'd have to eschew all elitism
and entitlement, preclude all
prima donna privilege,
demote all alpha individuals
to omega status for a change

we'd have to realize
that the line to be drawn
between ally and enemy
of the people can't be delineated
by gerrymandering genetics
gender or generation —
that until everyone joins
the ranks of the haves
the have nots will always exist
(the new haves will now just have to learn to share)

we'd have to learn
that if we're to trust anyone else —
and I don't see how we'll avoid that,
scientists armed with authentic objectivity
and the accumulated observations we call data
are a much better choice than anyone
who'd assert that it's money, politics
or faith that will save us
*(**none** of those have worked once
in all these thousands of years)*

we'd have to come to admit to ourselves
that peace officers and unionizers
are as essential as physicians and firefighters,
whose ranks need to be fortified – not forgone

but in The Fall of 2020
that was all some ways away –
pandemic and pandemonium still reigned

everyone had their eyes on the third
of November and the prospect
of an eventual vaccine

and Nero tweeted while Rome burned . . .

Days Of Infamy

01 Sep 1939
07 Dec 1941
06 Aug 1945
22 Nov 1963
04 Apr 1968
06 Jun 1968
08 Dec 1980
11 Sep 2001
06 Jan 2021

this is certainly not an exhaustive list —
these are just dates that almost everyone
who was alive at the time will remember

and of that last date (quite ironically),
most of you who fly the flag of the thin blue line
should be ashamed to admit that it was your Messiah
and his followers who not only trampled
that thin blue line, but attempted by thuggish force
to completely upend the democratic process
by physically stealing the voice of the people

never again will you be able to look us in the eye
and with *any* degree of honesty claim that you stand
for either law and order *or* democracy

5
Red Shift

Man, I'm Not Even Here

Looking back over my shoulder,
it sure seems as if I was there –
every there and then I've ever been.

But it never felt much like it when I *was* –
and it's not any different now.

I can see everyone moving – *in all three dimensions*
and every sound they make reverberates within me.

I feel their breathing and the coursing of their blood
and they seem to be vaguely aware of my presence
but I don't know what any of this really
looks or sounds like to them.

For all I know it could be nothing more
than fly-buzz in their ears.

There's a realness about them that I just
don't seem to possess, like I'm no more
than a ghost of someone who never really
even existed – a mere idea of what a life
could be like if there were only some way
to *genuinely* live it.

So here I am again it seems,
but it sure doesn't *feel* like it...

Out Here In The Bewilderness

it's an awfully big thing
to be contemplating,
especially when
you don't *seem* to need to

but if only they could see
what it all looks like from
deep down dark inside here . . .

Subsiding

to have shunned
the summer sun –
tried to stay out of it
as much as you
possibly could've
but for your labors
and the traffic
you couldn't escape

to take your comfort
in the dusk
and find your only refuge
in the anonymous
cloak of darkness,
the abbreviated night
where everyone
is more-or-less the same
because here the harshness
of the day can't beat us down
and remind us of our divergence

but what a difference
in these winter afternoons,
where you absorb all of the warmth
the fleeting daylight will allow

your thoughts will wander off
to trace the shadow-deepened
landscape, to scale the slopes
of mountains that rise abruptly from
these sprawling creosote scrublands

and you'll remember
everyone you ever knew
and wonder where they are
these years, if anywhere at all

Dichotomous?

for lifelong Paulette

If only I could comfort you.

If only I could make you understand.

And if it came down to a choice,
which one would you (I) choose?

October And Elsewhen

looking back across the decades,
it doesn't take too long to realize
there really only ever were two seasons –
October and the other eleven months

those three hundred thirty-four
days we must endure
in our plodding obligation to persist
so as not to disrespect
the heart, the lungs, the brain,
the bones and muscle, gristle, viscera
that have so long so far
so often seen us through

the deadwood-crackling bleak
wind-shivered winter on its way
to the foolish thin green hopefulness
of spring too soon brought low
and so mercilessly beaten down
to dust and perspiration
by the unrelenting sun

but then there comes October,
that long-longed-for month of months

and I could talk about the incandescent
yellow red de-greening of the trees,
the way your lungs will swell
in spite of you in amplifying air

I could talk about the bending of the light
in its deepening to amber, as each afternoon
grows shorter than the one that came before

or talk about the stirring restlessness,
the demise of summer's dawdle,
the urgent sense of preparation
for the onslaught of the frost

ah, but I've already said all that
in fall upon fall upon fall
and still it seems I haven't nailed it down

something still eludes me
in the way it plays against itself,
the frightening night of the living —
the commemorative day of the dead

I don't know why I can't
just let it rest
and lay this weary pen
down on these pages

I don't know why I can't
just go outside
and breathe it all in —
watch their wingbeats disappear
into the distant greying sky,
see all the colors draining
into brown and wait my turn
as some sixty-fourth October
slips away . . .

Some Wear In PST

10:37   in the thawing
afterfreeze
of a warm winter's
mid-morning
high and dry
in the Mojave

you can wonder
what went wrong –
what could be so bad
about being alive

you can bask
but for a moment
in the sugar-frosted
dread that some call hope

17:23   between the soothing
of the moon
and the impatience
of the wind,
the pastel pinkening
of clouds almost
defying gravity
and the deepening
of mountain
silhouescence

you can tune your weary ears
to the effervescent vespers
of house finches and
white-crowned sparrows
and consider what the
seasons must mean to them

21:09   in the low places
of the Earth
and all its darkness,
the alignment
of your thoughts
with the unevening
of feelings,

the distant dogbark
and the motordrone
of trucks out on
the highway,

a tentative accord
is somehow struck
between the wisdom
and the wear
the years impart

If Only For A Moment

in the dying of a tyrant
the implosion of an empire
built of broken bones
and bartered blood,
the bated breath of billions
who aren't allowed
to breathe the air
that billionaires
are bottling up for market

If Only For A Moment
in the virulence and violence
of have nots at war with have nots
set against each other
by those smiling other haves

If Only For A Moment
in the inequity of ethics
foisted by our forefathers
upon us –
so many in imagined entitlement
to something they've not earned
so many others claiming exemption
for themselves because of atrocities
suffered by someone else
they never even knew

If Only For A Moment
on the fourth day of November
in 2020's hind sight
we could rub our red-glared eyes
by the dawn's early light
and know another nightmare
was coming to an end

oh, if only for a moment...

Approaching Solstice

it's four o'clock,
the distant sun will all-too-soon
be swallowed by the mountains

as a rule I wouldn't miss it

but the shadows fall so long
upon these wind-worn weary
winter afternoons

and as I gaze across
the unrelenting desert
some three thousand
cold hard feet above the sea

the faltering of vision
and the flickering of thinking
notwithstanding

I can plainly feel the depths of Earth
that only years can plumb

Leaving Lapeer

late December 1972

You'd think we'd have all gotten used to it by now.

After all, we'd made this trip every year since 1958.

That's the year my older sister Paulette –
whose 8-year-old body had hopelessly
outgrown her 2-year-old mind – went to live at
Lapeer State Home and Training School.

Paulette seemed happy enough
as our visit drew to a close,
wearing her bright red new sweater
and having consumed a few of the cookies
Mom had baked for her.

In fact an oppressively hollow sense
of hopefulness pervaded the drafty
mop-washed halls, as if everyone there
was anticipating some nameless familiar
something that no one seemed to notice
had never actually arrived.

Such is the power of folklore I suppose –
the walls were gaily glittered
and there seemed to be enough
presents under the tree.

It was well past dark by the time we left
with at least a couple of hours back to Detroit.

My parents and my younger sister
and I each took our corner in the car,
Mom's smile slowly
went somewhere else
and we all just stared silently
into the distance.

Inside all was insulated warmth
courtesy of AM radio
and heater set to "defrost".

Outside was the cold and quiet night
drifting by our windows
in the diamond-pierced black sky
and mile upon mile of snowfields
punctuated every so often
by the brightly-colored farm house lights
the reindeer on the barn
or Mary, Joseph, Jesus
with their guests in the front yard.

I remember marveling at how
radiant heat and icy darkness
could coexist so side-by-side
separated only by
a quarter inch of glass –

and how all those joyous melodies
of angels, shepherds, wise men,
virgins, and messiahs
could so soaringly belie
the earthbound lonely emptiness
of such a winter's eve.

Thawlessness

there is an inner winter
that ravages the spirit
and chokes all thought
of spring

trees freeze
on the western horizon,
the silhouettes of memory
still standing black and hard
against the pastel pink
of weekly-bleakened dreams

with so little left to hope for now
you find your life-sustaining labors
more tedious than inspiring –
what is left but to persist?

darker than the day
and more luminous
than night

younger than
your yesteryears
and older
than the moment

even as the evening air
descends to silence those last
tits and twitterings of junco, finch,
and cardinal alike

the clattering of branches
lends a lonely rhythm
to the wind's hibernal hush

so many long cold
hours yet to pass,
you slump, trunk against
time-wearied trunk
and cup your ice-stung hands
around the moon…

After Ours

with cheese and jalapeño and olive the above

when the page is growing word-weary
and ink flows less profusely
now that night is wearing thin

when the blinds begin to bleed
those first invasive lumings of the dawn

and that last slice waits so greasily
to quell remaining growlings
of a hunger that's still burning deep inside

don't you wonder why you bother?

don't you wonder who'll be left
to even care to read this,
after all these hours
of yours and mine subside?

My little sister Carla left these three dimensions on 02 May 2021. Almost all of the poems in this book were written before we had any inkling of her illness. (She was diagnosed with stage 4 pancreatic cancer on 01 April 2021.)

Even as these pages go to press, I am rolling up my sleeves to dig deeply into the mounds of words that have piled up in her wake. I hope to meet all of you again in that next chapter maybe sometime late next year.

Until then, I wish you as much life as you can soak up – in both quantity and quality, in solitude and in communion with the rest who are left alive...

– Joseph Nicks, 24 December 2021

Appendix: a chronology of these poems

2019
Just A Poem	18 Apr
Terrestrial Anthr-apology	06 Sep
Nognosis	04 Dec

2020
For All That Lives And Eyes	01 Feb
Thawlessness	08 Mar
Dichotomous?	13 Apr
Another "We're All In This Together"	14 Apr
The Quiet Now	20 Apr
A Decade And A Day	24 Apr
After Ours	02 May
Walled-In Pond	09 May
Our Own Air Looms On The Horizon	09 May
No Wake Zone	09 May
Some Sequestered Questions	10 May
A Question Within A Question	10 May
According To Pall	29 May
The Great Equalizer	07 Jun
Post-prehensile	11 Jun
The Beleaguered Bleed Of Evening	15 Jun
The Endless Now	17 Jun
I Believe I Have The Floor	17 Jun
"Don't Let The Morning Come For Me"	18 Jun
The Fall	25 Jun
I Long For Longer Days	19 Jul
If Only For A Moment	21 Jul
The Fifteen Commandments Of Survival	02 Aug
Out Here In The Bewilderness	24 Aug
When	31 Aug
October And Elsewhen	18 Oct
Leaving Lapeer	24 Oct
Man, I'm Not Even Here	25 Oct

A Small Unswallowable Certainty	16 Nov
One Of These Nights	16 Nov
Some Wear In PST	17 Nov
Subsiding	19 Nov
I'd Like To Think	26 Nov
Approaching Solstice	14 Dec

2021

Days Upon Days	02 Mar
If You've Learned Anything At All	07 Jul
On Waking Up Again	11 Jul
Whose Cider You On?	27 Aug
Days Of Infamy	09 Nov
Manifest Density	18 Nov

THE AUTHOR

Since 1979, Detroit-born Joseph Nicks has divided his waking hours more-or-less equally between his "day job" and his nocturnal writing. The diurnal component has varied from manual laborer to water quality lab technician, assistant science advisor to a museum exhibits development team, technical writer, public school biology teacher, and field biologist.

He holds a B.S. in terrestrial zoology and two teaching credentials (multiple subject and biological sciences) and currently resides in the rural Mojave Desert. Recent publications include *Tales From The Otherground* (2014), *Can't Forget The Motor City...* (2018), and *this is boomslang* (2020).

Author photo: Luz Aguilar

www.ingramcontent.com/pod-product-compliance
Lightning Source LLC
Chambersburg PA
CBHW030915080526
44589CB00010B/316